Primary Geography

Teacher's Book 1 and 2 World around us

Stephen Scoffham | Colin Bridge

Geography in the primary school

Geography is the study of the Earth's surface. It helps children understand the human and physical forces which shape the environment. Children are naturally interested in their immediate surroundings. They also want to know about places beyond their direct experience. Geography is uniquely placed to satisfy this curiosity.

Geographical enquiries

Geography is an enquiry-led subject that seeks to answer fundamental questions such as:

- Where is this place?
- What is this place like (and why)?
- How and why is it changing?
- How does this place compare with other places?
- How and why are places connected?

These questions involve not only finding out about the natural processes which have shaped our environment, they also involve finding out how people have responded to them. Studying this interaction at a range of scales from the local to the global and asking questions about what is happening in the world around us lie at the heart of both academic and school geography.

Geographical perspectives

Geographical perspectives offer a uniquely powerful way of seeing the world. Since the time of the Ancient Greeks geographers have been attempting to chronicle and interpret their surroundings. One way of seeing links and connections is to think in terms of key ideas. Three concepts which geographers have found particularly useful in a range of settings are place, space and scale.

- Place focuses attention on the environment.
- Space focuses attention on location.
- Scale introduces a change in perspective that enables us to link the local and the global.

A layer of secondary concepts such as patterns, change and movement lie beneath these fundamental organising ideas and provide a way of further enhancing our understanding.

As they conduct their enquiries and investigations geographers make use of a number of specific skills. Foremost among these are mapwork and the ability to represent spatial information. The use of maps, charts, diagrams, tables, sketches and other cartographic techniques come under the more general heading of 'graphicacy' and are a distinguishing feature of geographical thinking. As more and more information has come to be represented electronically, the use of computers and other electronic applications has been championed by geography educators.

Geography in primary schools offers children from the earliest ages a fascinating window onto the contemporary world. The challenge for educators is to find ways of providing experiences and selecting content that will help children develop an increasingly deep understanding.

Collins Primary Geography

Collins Primary Geography is a complete programme for pupils in the primary school and can be used as a structure for teaching geography from ages 5-11. It consists of five pupil books and supporting teacher's guides with notes and copymasters. There is one pupil book at Key Stage 1 and four pupil books at Key Stage 2. There is also a supporting DVD for each Key Stage.

Aims

The overall aim of the programme is to inspire children with an enthusiasm for geography and to empower them as learners. The underlying principles include a commitment to international understanding in a more equitable world, a concern for the future welfare of the planet and a recognition that creativity, hope and optimism play a fundamental role in lasting learning. Three different dimensions – connecting to the environment, connecting to each other and connecting to ourselves – are explored throughout the programme in different contexts and at a range of scales. We believe that learning to think geographically in the broadest meaning of the term will help children make wise decisions in the future as they grow into adulthood.

Structure

Collins Primary Geography provides full coverage of the English National Curriculum requirements. Each pupil book covers a balanced range of themes and topics and includes case studies with a more precise focus:

- Book 1 and 2 *World around us* introduces pupils to the world at both a local and global scale.
- Book 3 *Investigation* encourages pupils to conduct their own research and enquiries.
- Book 4 *Movement* considers how movement affects the physical and human environment.
- Book 5 *Change* includes case studies on how places alter and develop.
- Book 6 *Issues* introduces more complex ideas to do with the environment and sustainability.

The programme is structured in such a way that key themes are revisited making it possible to investigate a specific topic in greater depth if required.

Investigations

Enquiries and investigations are an important part of pupils' work in primary geography. Asking questions and searching for answers can help children develop key knowledge, understanding and skills. Fieldwork is time consuming when it involves travelling to distant locations, but local area work can be equally effective. Many of the exercises in Collins Primary Geography focus on the classroom, school building and local environment. We believe that such activities can have a seminal role in promoting long term positive attitudes towards sustainability and the environment.

Lesson summary

Theme and lesson	Key idea	Story
Earth in space		
Introduction	Geography is about the world we live in.	
1 Earth, sun and moon	The sun and the moon move through the sky above the Earth.	Baby Squirrel's mistake
2 The planets	The Earth is one of eight planets which orbit the sun.	A journey in space
3 Day and night	As the Earth spins in space we get day and night.	Flying in the dark
4 Land and sea	Land and sea cover the Earth's surface.	Learning to dig
Planet Earth		
5 A living planet	Water brings life to the Earth.	A new life
6 The shape of the land	The land consists of mountains, hills and lowlands.	A journey to the sea
7 Volcanoes	Volcanoes bring hot rocks to the surface from deep underground.	Strange noises
8 World wonders	There are many beautiful things to see in the world.	A little bit of magic
Weather and seasons		
9 Experiencing the weather	There are many different types of weather.	A nasty surprise
10 Different types of weather	We can describe the weather using words and symbols.	Little Car's holiday
11 Extreme weather	Sometimes the weather can be wild and exciting.	A day off school!
12 The seasons	There is a pattern of seasons during the year.	Lazy Rufus
13 Going round the sun	The seasons change as the Earth goes round the sun.	The kittens can't agree
Local area		
14 Shelter	Homes give us warmth and shelter.	Camping in the garden
15 Houses around the world	People build houses in lots of different ways.	Town and country mouse

Lesson summary

Theme and lesson	Key idea	Story
16 Living in a village	People live together in groups or communities.	Max Mole loses his hat
17 Exploring local streets	There are lots of items in a street which help people live their lives.	The fancy dress party
18 Under your feet	The pipes and wires which are buried under the pavement provide the things we need in our daily lives.	Winnie tries to sleep
Maps and plans		
19 Maps and stories	Picture maps can show us about the places in songs and stories.	The Hare and the Tortoise
20 Treasure island	We can use maps to show places which are real or imagined.	A lucky find
21 Different plans	Plans show the shape of places around us.	A new school
22 The view from above	Plans show what places look like from above.	Hector Helicopter shows off
The UK		
23 UK countries	There are four countries in the UK.	Alfie tidies his room
24 UK mountains and rivers	The UK has mountains, rivers and lowlands.	Time for a story
Different environments		
25 Living in the arctic	The arctic is very cold and snowy.	Finding the right place
26 Living in the rainforest	The rainforest is hot and wet.	Polly Parrot loses her glasses
27 Living in the desert	Most deserts are very hot and very dry.	Stranded in the desert
28 Animals around the world	We share our world with many different plants and animals.	No story
World maps		
29 World continents	The world is divided into continents and oceans.	No story
30 World countries	There are about 200 countries in the world.	No story

Lesson planning

Collins Primary Geography has been designed to support both whole school and individual lesson planning. As you devise your schemes and work out lesson plans you may find it helpful to ask the following questions. For example, have you:

- Given children a range of entry points which will engage their enthusiasm and capture their imagination?
- Used a range of teaching strategies which cater for pupils who learn in different ways?
- Thought about using games as a way to enhance motivation?
- Explored the ways that stories or personal accounts might be integrated with the topic?
- Considered the opportunities for practical activities and fieldwork enquiries?
- Encouraged pupils to use globes and maps where appropriate?
- Considered whether to include a global dimension?
- Checked to see whether you are challenging rather than reinforcing stereotypes?
- Checked on links to suitable websites, particularly with respect to research?
- Made use of ICT to record findings or analyse information?

- Made links to other subjects where there is a natural overlap?
- Promoted geography alongside literacy skills, especially in talking and writing?
- Taken advantage of the opportunities for presentations and class displays?
- Ensured that the pupils are developing geographical skills and meaningful subject knowledge?
- Clarified the knowledge, skills and concepts that will underpin the lesson?
- Identified appropriate learning outcomes or given pupils the opportunity to identify their own ones?

These questions are offered as prompts which may help you to generate stimulating and lively lessons. There is clear evidence that when geography is fun and pupils enjoy what they are doing it can lead to lasting learning. Striking a balance between light-hearted delivery and serious intent is part of the craft of being a teacher.

Cross-curricular links

Collins Primary Geography can be easily linked with other subjects. The lessons on the Earth in space have natural synergies with themes from sciences, as do the lessons on the seasons, weather and environment. Local area studies overlap with work in history. The opportunities for promoting links with literacy are particularly strong. Stories are an ideal way of giving children the chance to develop reading and literacy skills in context. By making links of this kind it should prove possible to secure more time for geography than by teaching it as an discrete subject.

Studying the local area

The local area is the immediate vicinity around the school and the home. It consists of three different components: the school building, the school grounds, and local streets and buildings. By studying their local area, children will learn about the different features which make their environment distinctive and how it attains a specific character. When they are familiar with their own area, they will then be able to make meaningful comparisons with more distant places.

There are many opportunities to support the lessons outlined in *Collins Primary Geography* with practical local area work. First-hand experience is fundamental to good practice in geography teaching, is a clear requirement in the programme of study and has been highlighted in guidance to Ofsted inspectors. The local area can be used not only to develop ideas from human geography but also to illustrate physical and environmental themes. The checklist below illustrates some of the features which could be identified and studied.

Physical geography	Human geography
Hill, valley, cliff, mountain, rock, slope, soil, wood	Origins of settlements, land use and economic activity
River, stream, pond, lake, estuary, coast	House, cottage, terrace, flat, housing estate
Slopes, rock, soil, plants and other small-scale features	Roads, stations, harbours
	Shops, factories and offices
Local weather and site conditions	Fire, police, ambulance, health services
	Library, museum, park, leisure centre

All work in the local area involves collecting and analysing information. An important way in which this can be achieved is through the use of maps and plans. Other techniques include annotated drawings, bar charts, tables and reports. There will also be opportunities for the children to make presentations in class and perhaps to the rest of the class in assemblies.

Misconceptions

There is a growing body of research which helps practitioners to understand more about how children learn primary geography and the barriers and challenges that they commonly encounter. The way that young children assume that the physical environment was created by people was first highlighted by Jean Piaget. The importance and significance of early childhood misconceptions was further illuminated by Howard Gardner. More recent research has considered how children develop their understanding of maps and places. Children's ideas about other countries and their attitudes to other nationalities form another very important line of enquiry. Some key readings are listed in the references on page 11.

Differentiation

Collins Primary Geography sets out to provide access to the curriculum for children of all abilities. It is structured so that children can respond to and use the material in a variety of ways. Each lesson contains stimulus material which is designed to engage children imaginatively. Considerable emphasis is placed on verbal communication. The supporting copymasters provide opportunities for extension and development. Teachers will be able to select what they think will be appropriate from a range of resources. There is no need to work through all the material.

Differentiation by outcome

Each lesson starts with a brief introductory text which summarises a key idea in around 20-25 words. This is followed by a story, often involving an animal, which explores the main theme in a lighthearted but purposeful manner. Linked discussion questions explore the ideas further and provide an opportunity for structured talking. Younger children and slower learners may want to dwell on how the material relates to their own experience. More able children will be able to consider the underlying geographical concepts. The pace and range of the discussion can be controlled to suit the needs of the class or group.

Differentiation by task

The copymasters and activities which are suggested in the supporting notes can be modified according to the pupils' ability levels. Teachers may decide to complete some of the tasks as class exercises or help slower learners by working through the first part of an exercise with them. Classroom assistants could also work with individual children or small groups. More able children could be given extension tasks. Ideas and suggestions for extending each lesson are provided in the information on individual themes (pages 12-25).

Differentiation by process

Children of all abilities benefit from exploring their environment and experiencing the world around them at first hand. Work in the local area also helps to overcome the problems of written communication by focusing on concrete events. There could be opportunities for taking photographs as well as developing geographical vocabulary through observation and discussion.

The Geographical Association

The Geographical Association (GA) provides extensive support and advice for teachers including a range of excellent publications. The Barnaby Bear books, maps, posters and electronic resources are a popular way of helping young children learn about geography. *Superschemes Basics* and the *Geography Plus series* provide advice for teachers on lesson planning. Themes such as art, maps, outdoor learning and picture books provide the focus for the *Everyday Guides*. As well as holding an annual conference, the GA also produces a journal for primary practitioners, *Primary Geography*, which is published three times a year. To find out more and learn about the latest developments in geography education visit the website at www.geography.org.uk.

Assessment

Assessment is often seen as having two very different dimensions. Formative assessment is an on-going process which provides both pupils and teachers with information about the progress they are making in a piece of work. Summative assessment occurs at defined points in a child's learning and seeks to establish what they have learnt and how they are performing in relation both to their peers and to nationally agreed standards. *Collins Primary Geography* provides opportunities for both formative and summative assessment.

Formative assessment
- The discussion questions invite pupils to discuss a topic, relate it to their previous experience and consider any issues which may arise, thereby yielding information about their current knowledge and understanding.
- The activities and exercises focus will help pupils develop their geographical knowledge and understanding at a manner which is appropriate to their current level of ability
- The copymasters give pupils the chance to consolidate their ideas and extend their understanding of specific skills and themes.

Summative assessment
- Each lesson contains a panel which is designed to promote discussion. The questions provided here could be used summatively if required.
- The copymasters (see pages 30-59) will provide additional evidence of pupil achievement. Whether used formatively or summatively they are intended to broaden pupils' understanding.

Reporting to parents
Collins Primary Geography is structured around geographical skills, themes and places. As children work through the lessons they can build up a folder of work. This will provide evidence of mapwork and other practical activities both inside and outside the classroom and provide a rounded portrait of pupil achievement. This will also be a useful resource when teachers report to parents and show if a child is above average, satisfactory, or in need of help in geography.

National curriculum reporting
There is a single attainment target for geography and other National Curriculum subjects. This simply states that

> *'By the end of each key stage, pupils are expected to know, apply and understand the matters, skills and processes specified in the relevant programme of study.'*

This means that assessment need not be an onerous burden and that evidence of pupils' achievement can be built up over an entire Key Stage. The assessment process can also inform lesson planning. Establishing what pupils have demonstrably understood helps to highlight more clearly what they still need to learn.

Ofsted inspections

The regular reviews of geography teaching in the UK undertaken by Ofsted provide a clear guidance.

Ofsted recommendations

Ofsted recommends schools to:

- focus on developing pupils' core knowledge and sense of place.
- ensure that geography elements are clearly identified within topic based work.
- maximize opportunities for fieldwork in order to improve pupil motivation.
- make the most of new technology to enthuse pupils and provide immediacy and relevance.
- provide more opportunities for writing at length and focused reading.
- enable pupils to recognise their responsibilities as citizens.
- develop networks to share good practice.
- provide subject specific support and professional development opportunities for teachers.

Ofsted inspections

Ofsted inspections are designed to monitor standards of teaching in schools in England and Wales. Curriculum development is an on-going process and inspectors do not always expect to see totally completed programmes. What they are looking for is evidence of carefully planned strategies which are having a positive impact on the quality of teaching. However, inspectors must also note weaknesses and highlight aspects which need attention. If curriculum development is already in hand in your school, it should receive positive support. The following checklist provides prompts which may help prepare for inspections.

1 Identify a teacher who is responsible for developing the geography curriculum.
2 Provide a regular opportunity for discussing geography teaching in staff meetings.
3 See that all members of staff are familiar with the geography curriculum.
4 Decide how geography will fit into your whole school plan.
5 Make an audit of current geography teaching resources to identify gaps and weaknesses.
6 Discuss and develop a geography policy which includes statements on overall aims, topic planning, teaching methods, resources, assessment and recording.
7 Discuss the policy with the governors.
8 Devise an action plan for geography which includes an annual review procedure.

High quality geography

Primary Geography Quality Mark

The Primary Geography Quality Mark set up by the UK Geographical Association is another measure of excellence. This provides a self-assessment framework designed to help subject leaders. There are three categories of award. The 'bronze' level recognises that lively and enjoyable geography is happening in your school, the 'silver' level recognises excellence across the school and the 'gold' level recognises that excellence that is shared and embedded in the community beyond the school. The framework is divided into four separate cells (a) pupil progress and achievement (b) quality of teaching (c) behavior and relationships (d) leadership and management. For further details see www.geography.org.uk.

Achieving accreditation for geography in school is a useful way of badging achievements and identifying targets for future improvement. The Geographical Association provides a wide range of support to teachers to help with this process. In addition to an ambassador scheme and CPD sessions it produces a journal for primary schools, *Primary Geography*, three time a year. Other key sources are the Geographical Association website, the Primary *Geography Handbook* and books and guides for classroom use such as *Geography Plus*.

Finding time for geography

The pressures on the school timetable and the demands of the core subjects make it hard to secure adequate time for primary geography. However, finding ways of integrating geography with mathematics and literacy can be a creative way of increasing opportunities. Geography also has a natural place in a wide range of social studies and current affairs whether local or global. It can be developed through class assemblies and extra-curricular studies. Those who are committed to thinking geographically find a surprising number of ways of developing the subject whatever the accountability regime in which they operate.

References and further reading

Bonnett, A. (2009) *What is Geography?* London: Sage

Butt, G. (Ed.) (2011) *Geography, Education and the Future,* London: Continuum

Catling, S. and Willy, T. (2009) *Teaching Primary Geography*, Exeter: Learning Matters

DfE (2013) National Curriculum in England: Programmes of study – Key Stages 1 and 2 available at www.education.gov.uk/schools/teachingandlearning/curriculum/primary

Lucas, B. and Claxton, G. (2011) *New Kinds of Smart*, Maidenhead: Open University Press

Martin, F. (2006) *Teaching Geography in Primary Schools : Learning to live in the world*, Cambridge: Kington

Ofsted (2011) *Geography: Learning to Make a World of Difference*, London: Ofsted

Scoffham, S. (Ed.) (2010) *Primary Geography Handbook*, Sheffield: Geographical Association

Scoffham, S. (Ed.) (2013) *Teaching Geography Creatively*, London: Routledge

Wiegand, P. (2006) *Learning and Teaching with Maps*, London: Routledge

Information on the themes

Theme 1: Earth in space

Earth, sun and moon

The sun and the moon move through the sky above the Earth.

This lesson introduces children to Earth as an object in space. Like ancient people, young children tend to feel that the world revolves around them. Thinking about the sun and the moon is one way of enlarging their understanding. It also raises questions about how we calculate and account for time. The sun is the measure of the length of the day and the phases of the moon divides the year into months.

Story summary

Like many very young children, Baby Squirrel is rather nervous of the dark. Freddie Fox has realized this and decided to play a trick on her. He says that the moon is a ball in the sky which will fall if she closes her eyes at bedtime. Her mother sensibly points out that there is no danger. The moon has been orbiting the Earth since time began.

Using the story

Talk about beliefs that children have or have had which made them anxious. Why was Baby Squirrel frightened? Why does the moon look like a small ball in the sky? What stops it falling? Why is it a different colour to the Earth? What is the difference between a moon and a planet? Is the moon fixed up there or is it moving?

Picture books, tales and myths

Eliza and the Moonchild, Emma Chichester Clark, Andersen Press (2008)
The Way Back Home, Oliver Jeffers, HarperCollins (2007)

Activity

Ask the children to make a drawing of the Earth, sun and moon. They should then add labels.

The planets

The Earth is one of eight planets which orbit the sun.

The idea that the Earth orbits the sun was proposed by the Ancient Greeks but was not widely accepted until the sixteenth century. Similarly, while the inner planets (Mercury and Venus) were known by the Babylonians, Neptune and other more distant parts of the solar system have only been discovered in the last few hundred years. This lesson introduces children to the solar system and some of the differences between the planets.

Story summary

The Darins are a family of astronauts in the future. They are travelling from Earth out through the solar system, passing the planets on the way. Baby Oscar is learning to count and keeps trying his best but hasn't quite got it yet. Mum knows when to stop.

Using the story

The children will enjoy Baby Oscar's counting mistakes. In recounting correctly they will reinforce the number of planets in our solar system. They should appreciate that there are planets between Earth and the sun. Some children will enjoy learning more about the character of some of the planets and the special qualities of Earth.

Picture books, tales and myths

Adam's Amazing Space Adventure, Benji Bennett, Adam Printing Press (2009)
The Great Explorer, Chris Judge, Andersen (2012)

Activity

Make a mobile of the planets using discs of card, string and coat hangers for the frame.

Information on the themes

Day and night
As the Earth spins in space we get day and night.
The Earth spins on an axis marked by the North and South Poles. The Equator is an imaginary line around the Earth half way between the poles. This lesson introduces children to these key reference points. If you have access to a globe it will reinforce the material and illustrations in the pupil book.

Story summary
Sally Sparrow has become aware of the regularity of day and night. Sometimes certainty is a comfort but it can feel like being in a rut. Sally feels in a rut at the moment. However Brian Bat opens up the possibilities of enjoying the night rather than just sleeping. Sally decides on a change but doesn't enjoy the experience. However she is happier now to be a 'daytime' person.

Using the story
Talk about the way in which most plants and animals are adapted to either day or night. Look at how our lives in particular are ruled by this regular daily change. Although day and night is fixed there are seasonal changes to their length so Sally could look forward to doing different things at different times of year.

Picture books, tales and myths
I thought I Saw a Dinosaur, Emma Dodd, Templar (2007)
Apollo and the sun chariot (Greek myth)

Activity
Using match sticks and circles of card get the children to make spinning tops. This will illustrate how the axis remains stationary while other parts of the card are in motion.

Land and sea
Land and sea cover the Earth's surface.
The astronauts who travelled to the moon in the 1960s and 1970s were the first people ever to view the Earth from space. The photographs which they sent back captured both the fragility and unity of our world. Unlike other planets in the solar system, Earth is largely covered by water. Recognising the division between the oceans and the land provides the focus for this lesson.

Story summary
Max is the 'dominant male' among the mole family youngsters and of course thinks he knows it all. He sees his parents digging and is able to dig a little on his own. His father warns him that he needs more experience before setting off on his own but Max ignores him. At the first opportunity he is off. Unfortunately his excavations end up breaking through into water. He is rescued just in time.

Using the story
Talk about the life of a mole and how they dig through soil looking for worms. Max knew nothing about water and its properties. Emphasise how much water there is in our world and how we rely on the soil which is a thin layer and not even everywhere on Earth.

Picture books, tales and myths
Five Little Fiends, Sarah Dyer, Bloomsbury (2002)
The Crocodile Who Didn't Like Water, Gemma Merino, Macmillan Children's Books (2013)

Activity
Look carefully at a globe. Identify large blocks of land (continents) and islands around the coast. Get the children to name some of them.

Information on the themes

Theme 2: Planet Earth
A living planet
Water brings life to the Earth.
Although water covers large parts of the Earth's surface most of it is salty. Fresh water, which is essential for humans and many other forms of life, represents only about 2.5% of the total water on the planet. Much of this lies deep underground or is frozen in the polar ice caps. As human numbers and demand increases fresh water is becoming an increasingly scarce resource.

Story summary
Little Seed is typical of so many desert plants which hold life dormant for many years until a rare downpour of rain occurs. The water activates the seed which then has to go through a rapid lifecycle to produce more seeds in as short a time as possible. The Tumbleweed was partly inspirational for this story.

Using the story
The story is straightforward and direct but evocative of lifecycles and the significance of water. Talk about the lifecycle of plants with the children and if possible find a video sequence of a desert plant. Look at the way in which seeds hold life and wait for the right combination of water and warmth to trigger their development.

Picture books, tales and myths
The Drop in my Drink: The story of water on our planet, Meredith Hooper, Francis Lincoln (2011)
A Child's Garden, Michael Foreman Walker Books (2010)

Activity
Plant some mustard and cress seeds on a damp cloth to see how quickly they germinate and how they respond to water, warmth and light.

The shape of the land
The land consists of mountains, hills and lowlands.
The Earth's surface is constantly changing. As the tectonic plates move against each other mountains are built up and volcanoes come to the surface At the same time water, wind, ice and other forces wear away the land and try to reduce it to sea level. The interaction of these processes creates the landscapes we see today.

Story summary
Tommy is a young fish developing high in a mountain pond. He feels the natural urge to head for the sea. His benign surroundings lull him into a false sense of security about the journey. The river become wider and the current stronger. The landscape changes and there are dangers from waterfalls, humans and predators.

Using the story
Spend time discussing the environment at the beginning of the story; mountains and secluded, hidden pools. Why does Tommy experience a waterfall early in his journey? Why does the river get larger? What will he experience as he arrives at the sea?

Picture books, tales and myths
Oliver Who Travelled Far and Wide, Mara Bergman, Hodder Children's Books (2009)
From Kalamazoo to Timbuktu, Harriet Ziefert, Blue Apple Books (2005)

Activity
Find out the longest river and highest mountain in (a) the UK (b) the world.

Information on the themes

Volcanoes

Volcanoes bring hot rocks to the surface from deep underground.
There are approximate 1500 active volcanoes in the world. Around three-quarters of these are in what is known as the 'ring of fire' around the shores of the Pacific Ocean. Here tectonic plate movements bring molten magma to the surface. Children of all ages are fascinated by volcanoes. There will be opportunities to support this lesson with video footage. You may also find images of eruptions which are happening at the current time.

Story summary
In this humorous tale, Billy Bear reacts to the sounds produced by the enormous energy of an erupting volcano. The story is not intended to frighten children but the final paragraph picks up the fact that volcanoes are not to be taken lightly and people must react quickly when they become active.

Using the story
Billy Bear was living fairly close to a volcano. Where in the world might this be? There are mountains in the UK but none of them are active volcanoes. Explore the reasons for Billy's father deciding to move quickly out of the area. Volcanoes produce great quantities of poisonous gas and molten rock as well as a lot of noise.

Picture books, tales and myths
Gopher to the Rescue: A volcano discovery story, Terry Catasus Jennings, Abordale (2012)
Vulcan and his underground forge (Roman myth)

Activity
Make your own volcano model either as a class activity or with children working individually or in groups.

World wonders

There are many beautiful things to see in the world.
The seven wonders of the ancient world have found their place in history. Today people seek to protect landscapes and places which they particularly value by establishing nature reserves, national parks and heritage sites. Recognising that we live on a remarkable and very special planet is the central idea behind this lesson. Getting children to celebrate these wonders is an essential basis for caring about them in later life.

Story summary
This story has echoes of the Genie and the Lamp. Rose is walking along the beach on a grey day which reflects her sombre mood. Suddenly the waves wash up a bottle containing a genie who gives Rose three wishes. Her wishes produce a mighty iceberg, a cave with lovely stalactites and stalagmites and the glories of the Northern Lights. However, when she wishes for more toys she breaks the spell.

Using the story
Rose visits three outstanding natural creations. Talk about each one and the processes and timescales that produce them. What other wonders are there? What have the children experienced on holiday? Is there anything locally that might be considered a wonder? Can people create world wonders? Do they have to be big?

Picture books, tales and myths
How to Catch a Star, Oliver Jeffers, HarperCollins (2005)
My World, Your World, Melanie Walsh, Corgi (2004)

Activity
Collect some photographs of different 'wonders' for a class display.

Theme 3: Weather and seasons

Experiencing the weather

There are many different types of weather.

The sun provides the energy which drives the world's weather. The warmth of the air at the Equator contrasts with low temperatures at the poles. The wind seeks to equalise these differences in temperature and pressure. However, as the blows from place to place it also carries moisture which can result in cloud and rain We experience these changing conditions in daily and seasonal weather patterns.

Story summary

Freddie Fox sets off on a pleasant stroll on a bright day. However, the weather proves changeable. Ultimately a strong wind gets into his umbrella and he is deposited into a pond. The weather seemed pleasant to begin with but it wasn't in the end.

Using the story

Talk about how the weather affects our lives. Can you think of any times when you have been caught out by the weather? How does the weather affect the jobs which some grown-ups do? Freddie Fox complained that the weather wasn't being fair. Can the weather ever be fair?

Picture books, tales and myths

Rainy Day, Emma Haughton, Doubleday (2000)
The North Wind and the Sun,
  Brian Wildsmith (2007)

Activity

Set up a display table with clothes and items for different types of weather.

Different types of weather

We can describe the weather using words and symbols.

The UK enjoys a temperate climate with a great range of weather types, rarely very extreme. Weather changes, often within a short timescale, meaning that people have a great interest in weather forecasts. For succinctness and brevity a range of weather symbols has been developed and these are introduced here.

Story summary

Little Car sets out on holiday but is beset by a step by step deterioration in the weather. He is very optimistic about it changing and it does, but always for the worse. Annoyingly, when he is finally is forced to acknowledge that the weather has brought him to a complete stop, the sun comes out.

Using the story

Talk about all the different types of weather you can think of – snow, gales, showers with rainbows, heat-waves. How long does the weather stay the same? How do we find out what the weather is going to do next? Folklore offers one way of predicting the weather. Modern satellite images offer an alternative.

Picture books, tales and myths

Cloudy With a Chance of Meat Balls, Judi
  Barrett, Simon and Schuster (1978) (2008)
Stormy Weather, Debi Gliori, Bloomsbury (2010)

Activity

Make pictures to show different types of weather on Little Car's journey.

Information on the themes

Extreme weather

Sometimes the weather can be wild and exciting.
We are becoming increasingly aware of extreme weather. Better communications and increases in population mean that disasters are both more likely to happen and be better publicised when they do. There is also evidence that climate change is resulting in more unpredictable weather patterns. This lesson considers the power of nature but tries to avoid being alarmist. Extreme weather can be dramatic without being frightening.

Story summary
Fran Frog would like a change from school routines. She is disturbed in the night by a violent storm and wakes up next day to a flooded landscape. At least there won't be any school that day she thinks. However the teacher, ever resourceful, has decided to collect her pupils in a boat.

Using the story
The story introduces one type of extreme weather event in a way designed not to be worrying for young children. However the discussion could look at the implications of flooding and the impact that it has on people's lives. Extend the discussion to include other types of extreme weather both in UK and other parts of the world. The story of The Flood would provide a Biblical connection.

Picture books, myths and tales
The Storm Whale, Benji Davies, Simon and Schuster (2013)
After the Storm, Nick Butterworth, HarperCollins (2011)

Activity
Make a drawing of a storm with lightning.

Seasons

There is a pattern of seasons during the year.
The UK has four seasons of roughly equal length. The changes in weather and the hours of daylight have become ingrained in our lives. Seasonal celebrations such as Christmas, Easter and the summer Bank Holiday mark out the year. The school calendar still follows the pattern of the seasons as do many sporting events.

Story summary
This is a story with a traditional, folk tale basis. The profligate youngster enjoys the benefits of the benign conditions in spring and summer without preparing for the hard times to come. Rufus Rabbit reacts to the changes of autumn but has to seek help in winter. He promises to help the other rabbits in future but can he be trusted?

Using the story
Why did Rufus think he could live in a free and easy way? How did his behaviour change as the year went on? Why were the other rabbits making sure the underground home was in good condition? From the story, extract some characteristics for each season, the weather, temperature and effects on plants. How do plants and animals cope with winter? How are our lives affected by seasonal change?

Picture books, tales and myths
Persephone and pomegranate seeds (Greek myth)
The Selfish Giant, Oscar Wilde (1888)

Activity
Make some seasonal drawings for a class display or collage.

Information on the themes

Going round the sun

The seasons change as the Earth goes round the sun.

The previous lesson established the pattern of the seasons. This lesson explores what causes them. There is one main point which pupils need to understand. The Earth's axis, rather than being vertical, is tilted in relation to the sun. This means that over a period of a year places are tilted first towards and then away from the sun. The sun appears to move higher and lower in the sky as a consequence.

Story synopsis

The kittens are grumbling about the winter weather and wishing for summer. This leads to a discussion on why the seasons have to change. A variety of reasons are suggested, some more realistic than others.

Using the story

Discuss the children's own views about seasonal change and what they think of each kitten's suggestion in the order presented. This will reveal the extent of children's fanciful, even magical, ideas before they look at the diagram in the pupil book. Treat Father Christmas with care. Would he want to bother with the weather when he has his hands full with more important concerns?

Picture books, tales and myths

Going Round the Sun: Some planetary fun, Marianne Berkes, Dawn Publications (2008)

Activity

Spin a globe slowly and focus on the North Pole. Discuss the way that it has 24 hours of sunshine in summer and 24 hour darkness in winter.

Theme 4: Local areas

Shelter

Homes give us warmth and shelter.

All creatures need protection from weather, temperature and predators. Humans have developed the basic demands of shelter into sophisticated homes linked into complex systems supplying water, energy and communications. Air conditioning and central heating control the environment. However many people around the world are fortunate just to have basic shelter and protection.

Story summary

Becky and Matt are having fun in the garden. It's warm and sunny and the prospect of camping out at night seems an adventure. Their mother knows that a tent is not as protective as it seems but the children are determined to go ahead. They set up their tent as a little home but are back inside the house when the noises of the night keep them awake.

Using the story

Why do Becky and Matt think their tent is like a little home? What did they put in it to make them think they could stay out overnight? Discuss what worried the children in the night. Should they have been worried? These noises are there every night. Why don't the children worry about them when they are in their bedrooms?

Picture books, tales and myths

A Place to Call Home, Alexis Deacon, Walker Books (2011)
The three little pigs

Activity

Make your own house models from strips of light card. Fold the card into three sections to form the walls and floor. Use a second piece of card for the roof. Draw the doors and windows.

Information on the themes

Houses around the world

People build houses in lots of different ways.
Traditionally houses were built from local resources such as wood, stone, thatch and clay. In the last few hundred years the Industrial Revolution and the development of roads and railways have made it possible to transport building materials from one place to another. Now new materials such as plastic, glass and concrete have heralded further developments. Despite these changes house styles still needs to respond to local weather conditions and financial constraints. There are also increasing attempts to make new houses carbon neutral.

Story summary
This story is based on the traditional tale about the town mouse and the country mouse. Bill Mouse takes his cousin Rita around the village and its houses. Rita finds country life rather slow and takes Bill back to the city. He sees all the buildings but the pace of life is too hectic and he thankfully returns home.

Using the story
Discuss the differences between a village and a city, especially the numbers of people who might live in each place. How does this affect the homes that are found there? Think of the basic sorts of building materials used in old houses in the UK and other parts of the world. How do they differ from modern houses? Why weren't they all the same?

Picture books, tales and myths
The House at Pooh Corner,
  A. A. Milne, Egmont (1928) (2013)
The fisherman and his wife (Grimm's fairy tales)

Activity
Go for a short walk to look at different houses in your area. See how many different types of building material you can find.

Living in a village

People live together in groups or communities.
A village is the basic settlement which from early times has enabled people to settle in one place instead of roaming nomadically. Villages need a water supply for drinking and washing and countryside to produce food. Critically they also provide other resources for a sustainable lifestyle. People specialise in different tasks and provide each other with social support. A village is a community.

Story summary
Max Mole has lost his hat and can't find it anywhere. He is hampered in his search because, like many other moles, he has rather poor eyesight. Max wanders around the village going from place to place. Finally he goes to the school. When he asks the children the right question they tell him where to find his hat.

Using the story
Talk about the places Max Mole visits as he searches round the village. What jobs and activities go on in each one? Would children like to live in an isolated house in the country? What is it that makes a community?

Picture books, tales and myths
Katie Morag Delivers the Mail, Mairi
  Hedderwick, Red Fox (2010)

Activity
Make a class display of a village. This could either consist of pictures of buildings and features arranged around a street plan or models set out on a display table.

Information on the themes

Exploring local streets

There are lots of items in a street which help people live their lives.
The items which are added to a street to make it habitable are known as street furniture. There is a great variety of street furniture including benches, bus stops, post boxes, telephone kiosks, road signs and litter bins. This lesson alerts children to the range of items in their local environment and helps them to question why each one is needed.

Story summary
William is excitedly rushing to a fancy dress party dressed as a pirate. Unfortunately in the crowded street he bumps into various items of street furniture; a litter bin, bus stop, lamp post and a drain. His costume is spoiled but all is not lost. He appears to make a very good scarecrow.

Using the story
What did William bump into and why were those things there? Where does litter go?

Where do the buses come from? How do the lights work? What other things might he have bumped into (bollards, telephone poles, post boxes, signposts)?

Picture books, tales and myths
Belonging, Jennie Baker, Walker Books (2004)

Activity
Take photographs for a display about the things in the streets around your school. See if you can find something for different letters of the alphabet.

Under your feet

There are lots of pipes and wires under the pavement.
Streets are full of clues to the systems that sustain modern lifestyles. Water, electricity, telephone and gas are supplied to nearly every home and rubbish and waste water are removed without fuss. These services link us to places beyond the local area which we depend on for survival. Without them it would be impossible for people to live clustered together in towns and cities. The lids and covers in the pavement provide evidence of different services which children can consider and explore.

Story summary
Winnie the Worm has been tunnelling through the soil as usual. She decides to take a rest. Unfortunately it is a busy moment above ground. She is woken by a series of drills installing various underground pipes and cables for water, gas and electricity. Belatedly Max Mole turns up with some earplugs.

Using the story
Talk about the way in which worms constantly travel through the ground, their tunnels aerating the soil and providing air and drainage for plant roots. Why do the other things need to be underground? Where are the pipes and cables going to? Where have they come from? What is the difference between a pipe and a cable? What would life be like without them?

Picture books, tales and myths
Superworm, Julia Donaldson, Alison Green Books (2012)

Activity
Make a set of rubbings of lids and covers in the pavements around your school.

Information on the themes

Theme 5: Maps and plans

Maps and stories

Picture maps can show us about the places in songs and stories.
Nearly every story is set in a place or location and many involve a journey of some kind or other which can be mapped. Maps can take a wide variety of forms. The simplest maps are simply pictures of places. This lesson aims to introduce children to maps in a way that relates to their interest and understanding. You might even decide not to use the word 'map' but to talk about 'pictures' instead.

Story summary

This story is a retelling of Aesop's fable of the Hare and the Tortoise. The hare is boastful and erratic. The tortoise is quiet and plodding. These two different characters decide to prove their qualities in a race. The hare ought to win without difficulty but it is the tortoise that reaches the winning post first.

Using the story

Talk through the story and act it out with the children before asking them to draw their own picture maps of the race. They will need to show the different landmarks such as the tree, grassy bank and lettuce field. They could add other features of their own. There are opportunities to make a collage.

Picture books, tales and myths

The Hare and the Tortoise, Brian Wildsmith, Oxford (2007)

Activity

Make a class display to illustrate the places and events in a different story or song.

Treasure island

We use maps to show places both real and imagined.
Maps have great power because they are a record of the lie of the land and therefore enable us to travel and make journeys without getting lost. In this lesson children explore how maps and compass directions enable us to find places and objects. The idea of buried treasure will stimulate imaginative responses. As you talk about the map you might think about treasures in a broader sense to include buildings, plants and landscapes.

Story summary

Tom and Karen are excited because their father has brought a metal detector. Sam next door is jealous and produces a spurious treasure map to send them off on a wild goose chase. The children navigate around the island without success until, much to Sam's disgust, they find some 'treasure' near the castle.

Using the story

Talk about the things which are shown on the map and the different landscape features. Have any of the children visited an island? What was it like? Follow the children's journey on the map. This will involve a discussion about compass directions and might lead to finding out about compass directions in and around your school.

Picture books, tales and myths

Rosie's Magic Horse, Russell Hoban, Walker Books (2012)

Activity

Get the children to make their map of an imaginary island or place. Older pupils might devise directions for finding treasure.

Information on the themes

Different plans

Plans show the shape of places around us.

Plans show small areas in great detail, while maps show larger areas in a more generalised way. Plans are particularly important to builders and architects who use them to visualise different areas and spaces. Children may be introduced to plans from an early age. They relate particularly well to plans of familiar places where they are able to identify familiar features. Contrasting the side view (elevation) with the overhead view (plan) can be an interesting exercise.

Story summary

The children are excited because they have a new school. The builder promises that it will be built in a surprisingly short time. The opening day arrives and the children go in class by class, the youngest first. Class 1 is very happy, but the other classes can't fit in. The head teacher and the secretary complain that their rooms are too big. The builder explains that the building was ready quickly because all the rooms are the same size. He is not popular.

Using the story

Analyse the story and discuss why everyone is unhappy with the building except Class 1.

Think about your own building. Try and draw a big plan. It does not have to be particularly accurate or to scale, but should reflect the children's conceptual view of the room sizes and how they think the school is arranged.

Picture books, tales and myths

Percy's Bumpy Ride, Nick Butterworth, HarperCollins (2011)

Activity

Select some familiar items such as bottles, cartons and containers. Ask the children to draw round the base to create the plan. See if they can they match the items to their plans once they have been separated.

The view from above

Plans show what places look like from above.

Although there are no set rules, maps and plans are often drawn from above. Taking an overhead view solves the problem of perspective but the shapes which are revealed are often unfamiliar. With increasing height the representation tends to become even more abstract. Making comparisons with overhead photographs helps to bring back a measure of 'reality'.

Story summary

Hector Helicopter thinks he knows it all. Because he's always looking down on things he thinks he knows the shape of everything. There are playing fields and roundabouts and lots of squares. He needs to land to refuel. Unfortunately he confuses his square landing pad with the roof of a square tower block.

Using the story

Talk about what Hector Helicopter has discovered about the plan view of buildings and places. How did Hector come to make his mistake? Can the children think of other examples that Hector might have seen of rectangles, circles and squares? Make plan views of objects in the classroom. What parts of the school might be squares, rectangles or circles?

Picture books, tales and myths

A Balloon for Grandad, Nigel Gray, Orchard Books (2002)

Zoom, Istvan Banyai, Viking Kestrel (2007)

Activity

Compare maps and aerial photographs of your school and its surrounding area.

Theme 6: The UK

UK Countries

There are four countries in the UK.

The UK consists of four countries which have amalgamated over hundreds of years. England and Wales were brought together in 1284, Scotland joined the union in 1707 and Northern Ireland was added in 1921. Thinking of the UK as separate countries sometimes creates confusion. This lesson aims to help children name and locate the different areas.

Story summary

Alfie is annoyed when his father asks him to tidy his room. He wishes he could be somewhere far away. A mysterious wizard grants his wish and he finds himself first in Scotland, then in Northern Ireland and finally in Wales. None of these places really suits him and he decides his home back in England is best. But he still hasn't tidied his room.

Using the story

Discuss where Alfie is to start with and the sequence of the places he visits. What is special about each of the places he visits? Find out how many children have been to different countries of the UK? What impressions and memories do they have? Do they associate the different countries with particular sports, foods or landscapes?

Picture book, tales and myths

Katie in London, James Mayhew, Orchard Books (2004)

We Are Britain!, Poems by Benjamin Zephaniah, Frances Lincoln (2003)

Activity

Divide the children into four groups – one for each country of the UK. Get them to find out all the things they can about their area.

UK mountains and rivers

The UK has mountains, rivers and lowlands.

The UK has a remarkably varied landscape. Scotland is famous for its mountains and lochs, England has lowlands and hills, Wales is known for its valleys and Northern Ireland for its green fields. The rocks beneath the surface are one of the reasons for these different landscapes. The erosion which occurred during the last ice age is another factor.

Story summary

Mrs Jones is looking forward to telling the children about different places in the UK. She gives the children a number of options. There are stories about the Snowdon mountain railway, wildlife in the River Severn or an adventure on the Norfolk Broads. The children refuse them all so they end up doing sums.

Using the story

The story focuses on three different landscapes - mountains, rivers and lowlands. Talk about their different characteristics. Have any children been climbing in the Welsh mountains or been boating in the Norfolk Broads? What other places do they know of? What makes each one special?

Picture books, tales and myths

ABC UK, James Dunn, Francis Lincoln Children's Books (2009)

Activity

Create a wall display about the UK. Get the children to make drawings of different features to add to a poster or your own outline map of the UK.

Information on the themes

Theme 7: Different environments

Living in the arctic

The arctic is very cold and snowy.

The arctic has one of the coldest and harshest climates on Earth. Around the North Pole the ocean is covered by pack ice for most of the year. Around the shores an area of marshes, lakes and peat bogs forms a frozen wilderness known as the tundra. Creatures like the polar bear have evolved to survive in these conditions. Now that the ice is melting due to global warming they are losing their habitat.

Story summary

The bear, the walrus and the reindeer are having a discussion. They are bored with their daily lot and decide to swap places. They soon find themselves even worse off and return to their familiar territories.

Using the story

The story describes some major features of the arctic–snow, sea, land with limited vegetation such as moss, and fish. The story highlights the lack of variety in a landscape which might be unchanging over huge areas. Why could the animals not successfully swap places? What might it be like for humans to live in the arctic?

Picture books, tales and myths

Polly and the North Star, Polly Horner, Orion Children's Books (2002)

Winnie the Pooh (An Expotition to the North Pole), A.A. Milne, Egmont (2013)

Activity

Find out about other creatures that live in the arctic. Get the children to add photographs and make drawings as part of an extended study.

Living in the rainforest

The rainforest is hot and wet.

Tropical rainforests are hot and damp with intensive tree cover. This environment encourages a multitude of life. The rainforest only covers 6% of the Earth's land surface yet contains more than half of the world's plant and animal species. The trees also put moisture into the air which regulates the world's climate. As the forests are cleared it is leading to irreversible changes.

Story summary

Polly Parrot is having a difficult day. She has lost her glasses. She searches for them in the forest mistaking a variety of plants and creatures. Finally the spectacles are returned by her sister. Polly had mistakenly included them in a birthday parcel.

Using the story

List all the plants and creatures that Polly meets. How does the list differ from plants and creatures in the UK? Imagine what life would be like in the rainforest. Make up stories for the other creatures and what might happen to them amongst the trees.

Picture books, tales and myths

We're Roaming in the Rainforest, Laurie Krebs, Barefoot Books (2010)

Activity

Fold a piece of paper or card down the middle like a greetings card. Draw rainforest trees and plants on the front. Draw rainforest creatures inside.

Information on the themes

Living in the desert
Most deserts are very hot and very dry.
Australia is the driest inhabited continent. The deserts make up most of the outback in the central areas. In the past the deserts were seen as inhospitable places. Now people can visit the amazing scenery and see the rocks, gorges and coloured sands using powerful, modern vehicles. These fragile ecosystems are vulnerable to increased human access.

Story summary
Kate Koala decides to explore the Australian desert. She is warned about the dangers and what best to do if the car breaks down. The desert is bigger than she imagined and she runs out of petrol. She sends a message for help with a passing kangaroo but it leads to confusion.

Using the story
Talk about what children think makes a desert. Some are very sandy but most, like the Australian outback, have a varied, rocky terrain.

The key is they are very dry and often very hot. What would Kate see and why would people want to explore the desert? What would you take if you were setting off on a desert tour?

Picture books, tales and myths
Just-So Stories (How the Camel Got His Hump), Rudyard Kipling, Oxford (1902), (2009)

Activity
Create a desert environment using a sand tray and small drawings and models of different plants and creatures.

Animals around the world
We share our world with many different plants and animals.
Over a period of 4000 million years a great diversity of plant and animal life has evolved on Earth. However, pressure of human numbers and loss of habitat is leading to mass extinctions. Helping children to celebrate the diversity of creation may encourage them to want to care for it as they grow older.

Picture books, tales and myths
The Trouble with Dragons, Debi Gliori, Bloomsbury (2008)
The Snail and the Whale, Julia Donaldson, Macmillan Children's Books (2003)
Babar's World Tour, Laurent de Brunhoff, Harry N Abrams (2005)

Theme 8: World maps

World continents
The world is divided into continents and oceans.
Continents and oceans are very large units which provide a general framework that enables us to make sense of the world. However, they are not without problems. It is difficult to be precise about where an ocean begins and ends. Continents too tend to merge into each other. Islands create special difficulties. This lesson provides children with a map which will help make sense of the basic divisions.

World countries
There are nearly 200 countries in the world.
Young children sometimes find it difficult to distinguish between countries and continents. This lesson explores how continents are broken into smaller units. A country can be defined as a territory which has its own flag and laws. They vary enormously in size. Six countries are highlighted in this spread. Pupils might want to learn about other countries as an extension activity.

Copymaster matrix

Copymaster	Description
Earth in space	
Earth, sun and moon	Children colour pictures of the Earth, sun and moon and add labels.
The planets	Starting with a colour code, children colour the sun and planets.
Day and night	Pupils colour a globe and make pictures to show day and night.
Land and sea	A simple exercise in which children identify land and sea on a globe.
Planet Earth	
A living planet	Children colour drawings to show a sequence in plant growth.
The shape of the land	Children colour a landscape picture and make a list of words to describe it.
Volcanoes	A practical activity in which children create their own model volcanoes.
World wonders	Children colour three outline drawings of world wonders before making a drawing of their own.
Weather and seasons	
Experiencing the weather	Children label drawings of different types of weather.
Different types of weather	Pupils colour weather words and symbols and cut them out for a game of weather snap.
Extreme weather	An open-ended activity in which children make their own extreme weather picture.
The seasons	Children colour a dial to link the seasons to the months of the year.
Going round the sun	Children colour and think about diagrams showing the Earth in relation to the sun's rays in winter and summer.
Local areas	
Shelter	A modelling activity in which pupils create a simple house.
Houses around the world	Children colour and label drawings of different house types.

Aim	Teaching points
To introduce children to two objects which dominate the sky and which provide the basis for our notion of time.	Being egotistical, young children sometimes think the sun and the moon follow them around.
To identify Earth's position in the solar system as one of eight planets of differing sizes.	See that the pupils understand that some planets are much larger than others and that some, like Mars and Neptune, have a distinctive colour.
To help children understand that day and night are caused by the spinning of the Earth.	The globe is shown tilted at an angle to the sun's rays as it is in reality.
To illustrate that sea covers large parts of the Earth's surface.	See that pupils can identify the UK and distinguish between land and sea before they start this activity.
To show that plants need water and sunlight in order to grow.	When they add the arrows pupils will be creating a simple flow line diagram illustrating a sequence.
To build up children's landscape vocabulary.	Depending on their ability the children could either write down the words or discuss them amongst themselves.
To help pupils understand the basic structure of a volcano.	Pupils will need scissors and glue for this activity – for the best results duplicate the copy master on light card.
To introduce the idea that we live on a remarkable planet of great beauty and variety.	Pupils could either make their own drawings directly from the pupil book or research their own examples.
To consider how the weather changes and the way that it affects us.	This theme links well with picture book stories and could lead to a large class weather display.
To introduce pupils to symbols in a way that they can relate to and understand.	Pupils will need to cut out the cards and will need to be organised into small groups to play the game.
To explore dramatic and powerful weather events in a non-threatening way.	As well as making a drawing, children are asked to do some simple writing in this activity.
To establish the sequence of the seasons using a graphical device.	Some children may have difficulty reading the names of the seasons and months of the year.
To illustrate how the tilt of the Earth's axis causes seasons to change.	Children need to understand that the sun rises and falls with the seasons but understanding the causes can be revisited as they become older.
To generate models which can be used in a class display.	Make a sample model of your own to show the class and consider enlarging the copy master to A3 size.
To compare and contrast different house designs.	You could extend this activity by setting up a display of photographs different houses from magazines and the internet.

Copymaster matrix

Copymaster	Description
Living in a village	Children annotate a drawing of a small village.
Exploring local streets	A survey sheet to help pupils record findings from a streetwork study.
Under our feet	Children construct a small model of a street showing pipes and wires under the roadway.
Maps and plans	
Maps and stories	Children complete a drawing showing the route taken by the Hare and the Tortoise.
Treasure island	An exercise in which children identify the grid squares of different features.
Different plans	Children associate drawings of buildings with their plan shapes.
The view from above	Children create their own map of a real or imagined place.
The UK	
UK countries	Children colour a flag and add labels to an outline map.
UK mountains and rivers	Children complete a map showing landscape features and turn it into a jigsaw.
Different environments	
Living in the arctic	Children colour drawings of different plants and animals.
Living in the rainforest	Children colour drawings of rainforest creatures and add them to a larger picture.
Living in the desert	Pupils complete drawings for a desert mobile.
Around the world	
Animals around the world	Children join the dots to create drawings of creatures then fill in an animal crossword.
World continents	Children colour a world map using the colours specified in a key.
World countries	Working from the pupil book children colour flags of different countries.

Aim	Teaching points
To explore the range of facilities that can be found in a village.	See that pupils identify the inn (with sign outside) and the shop next to it before they begin.
To focus attention on the range of services which cater for people's needs	The drawings on the sheet will not exactly match the examples that you find locally.
To illustrate in three dimensions the range of services which reach us by travelling under the ground.	Explain to the children that some of the drawings appear upside down as the model needs to be folded.
To draw attention to landmarks and the sequence in which they appear.	Pupils could add to the 'spectators' by making drawings of other animals.
To develop understanding of alpha-numeric grids.	See that the children understand that the letter comes first and the number comes second.
To introduce the notion of plan perspectives at a scale pupils can comprehend.	Making plans of toys is an excellent way both to introduce and reinforce this activity.
To practice using maps and to show how grid squares can support map making.	Discuss with pupils what they want to show on their maps so that they rehearse what they are doing before they start.
To show the four countries of the UK.	The children could see how the maps they have created compare with atlas maps.
To consolidate knowledge and understanding of the UK landscape.	It will help if the pupils have coloured round the coast in blue before they create the jigsaw.
To introduce pupils to the distinct flora and fauna of the arctic.	Pupils could cut out their drawings for a class display.
To explore some of the unique features of the rainforest habitat.	Pupils will need to draw a rainforest scene before they start to add their animals.
To focus attention on desert plants and creatures.	Talk about how different plants and creatures manage to live in the desert climate.
To draw attention to the flagship species which live in different parts of the world.	The children might like to devise their own dot to dot drawings of other familiar creatures.
To show the different continents on a world map.	See that the children understand that islands form part of some continents, especially in Southeast Asia.
To help children understand that there are lots of different countries in the world.	See that the children look carefully at the flags they are copying rather than guessing at the design and colours.

1. Colour the picture of the Earth, sun and moon.
2. Add labels to your drawing.

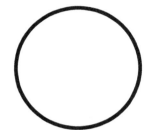

m _ _ _

E _ _ _ _

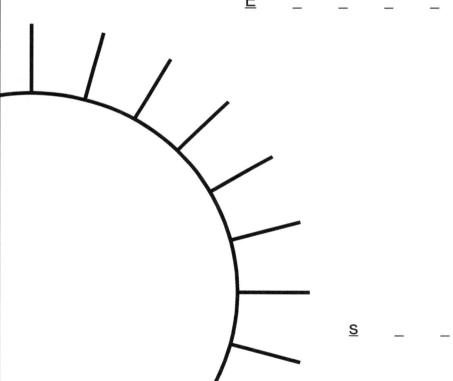

s _ _

1. Colour the boxes. Use a different colour for each planet.

2. Now use the same colour in the picture.

Planet	Colour	Planet	Colour
1 Mercury	pink	5 Jupiter	brown
2 Venus	orange	6 Saturn	yellow
3 Earth	green	7 Uranus	blue
4 Mars	red	8 Neptune	black

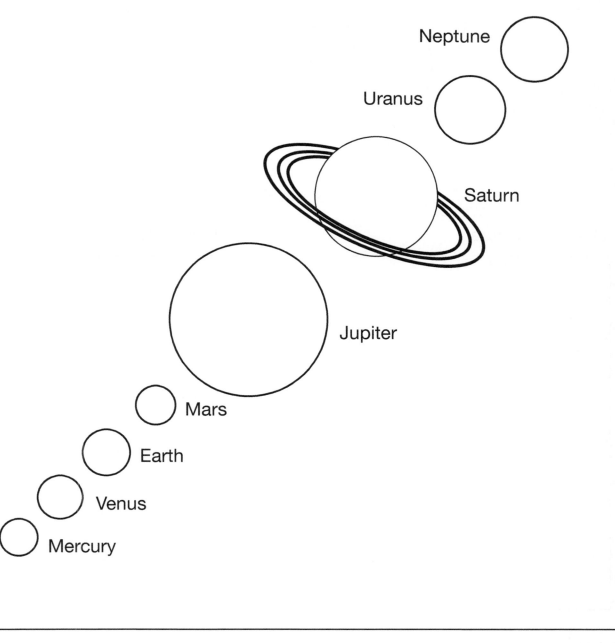

③ Day and night

1. Colour the globe to show day and night.

2. Draw a day time picture and a night time picture.

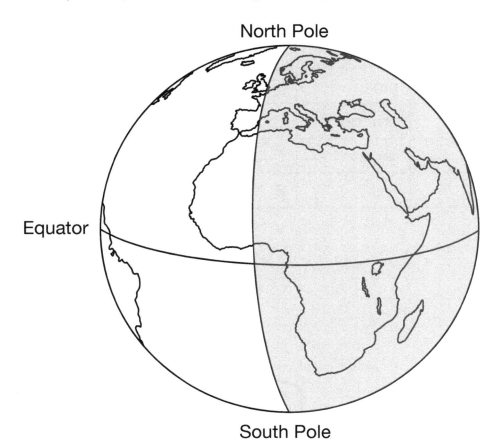

North Pole

Equator

South Pole

Day time picture

Night time picture

Land and sea

1. Colour the boxes in the key.

2. Colour the map of the world using these colours.

Key

green	land
blue	sea

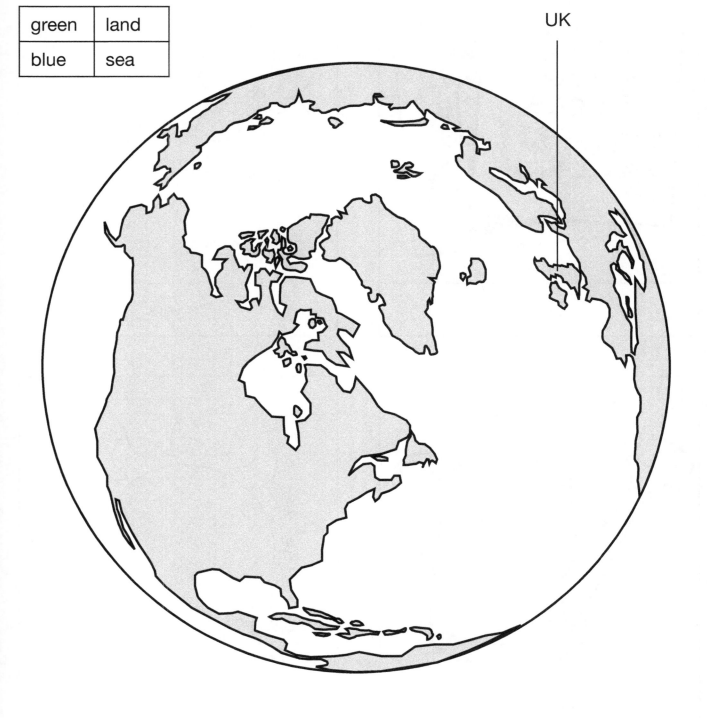

UK

Name ....

1. Colour the drawings.

2. Draw arrows linking the drawings in the correct order.

seeds

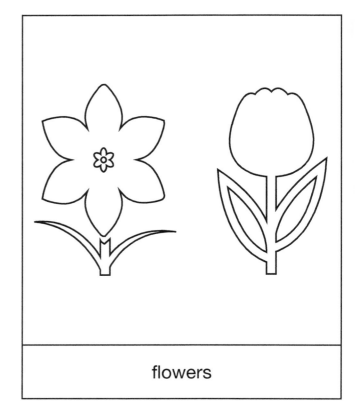

flowers

water

sun

6 The shape of the land

Name ....

1. Colour the drawings. **2.** Cut along the dotted lines.

3. Put the picture together again.

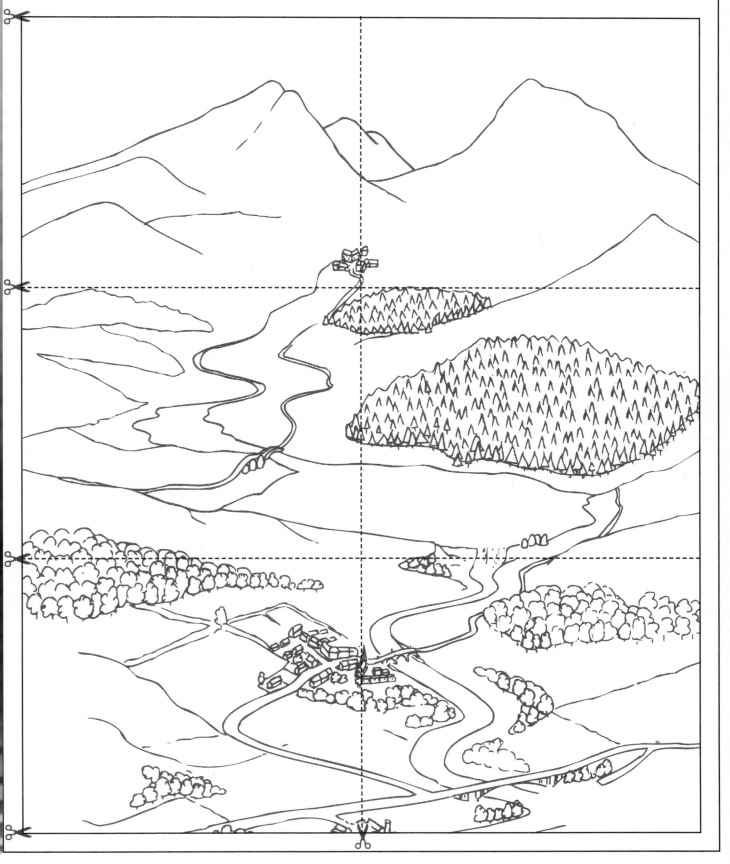

Name ....

1. Colour the model. 2. Cut round the edge.

3. Stick down the flap to make a cone.

4. Add smoke using tissue paper
   or cotton wool.

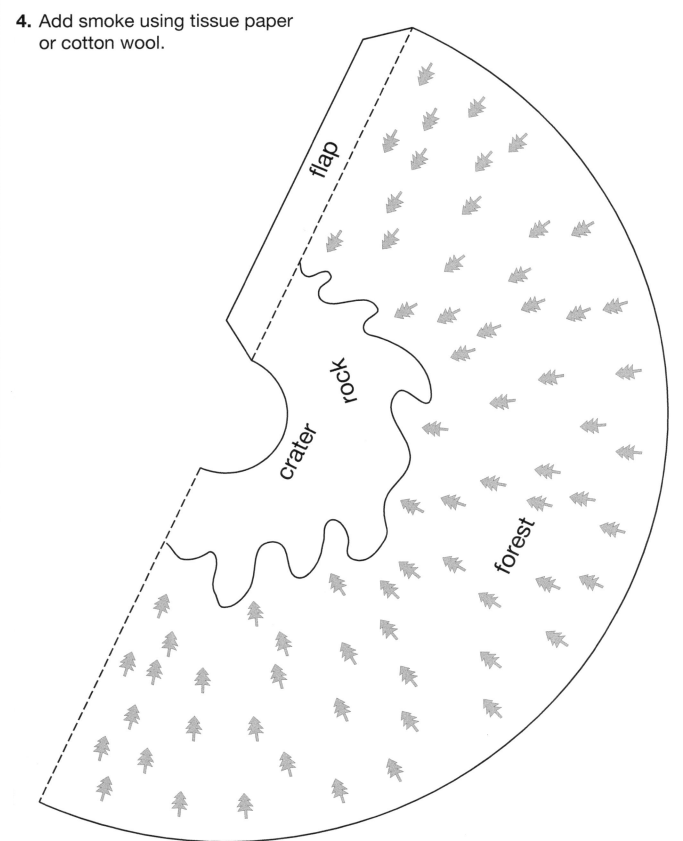

Name ....

1. Colour the pictures of the different wonders.

2. Make your own drawing of a world wonder in the empty box.

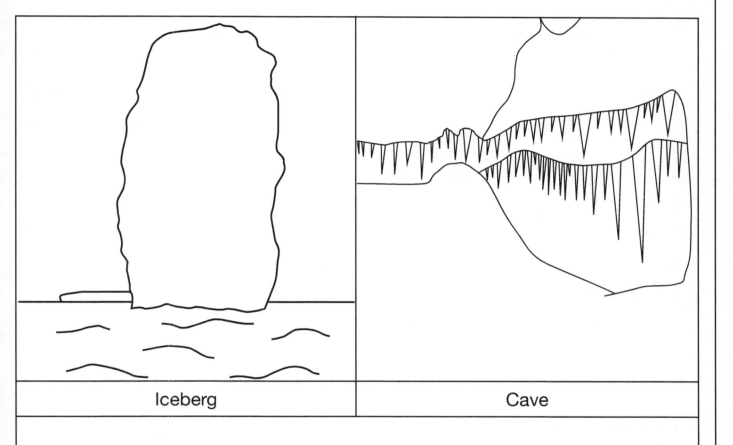

| Iceberg | Cave |

1. Label the pictures with these weather words.

   hot   cold   wet   windy

2. Colour the pictures.

Name ....

1. Colour the pictures.

2. Cut out the words and pictures.

3. Play a game of weather snap with a group of other children.

snowy

rainy

cloudy

sunny

windy

stormy

11 Extreme weather

1. Make your own extreme weather picture in the space below.

2. Write a few words saying what your picture shows.

My picture shows ....

....

....

....

12 The seasons

Name ....

1. Write the name of each season round the edge of the dial.

2. Colour the dial and weather symbols.

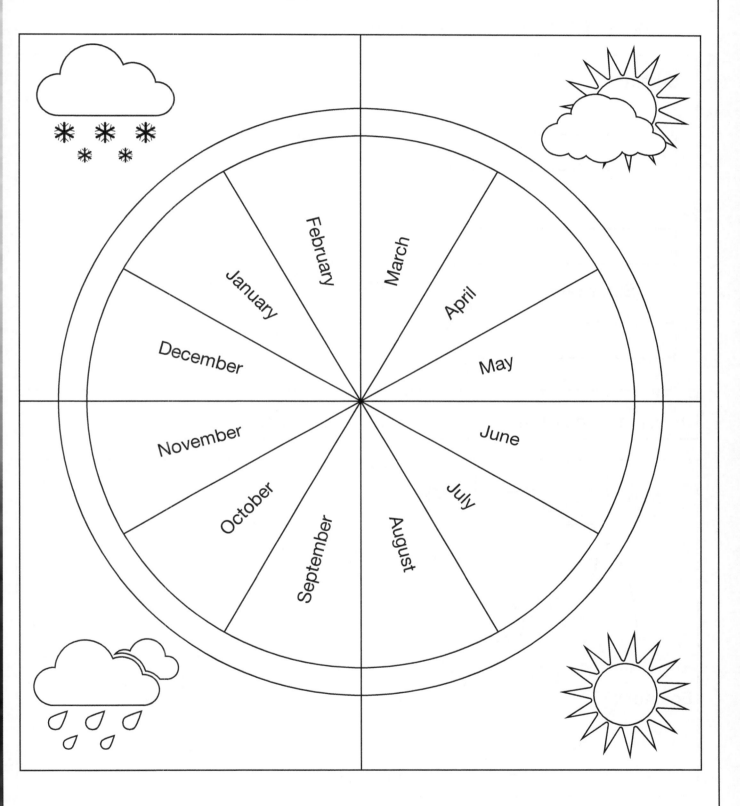

🕐 Going round the sun

Name ....

1. Colour the pictures.

2. Finish the sentences using the best words.

   towards the sun   away from the sun

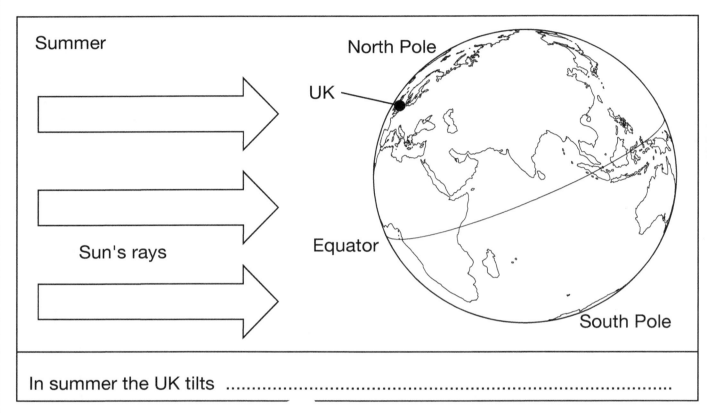

Summer

Sun's rays

North Pole

UK

Equator

South Pole

In summer the UK tilts ....

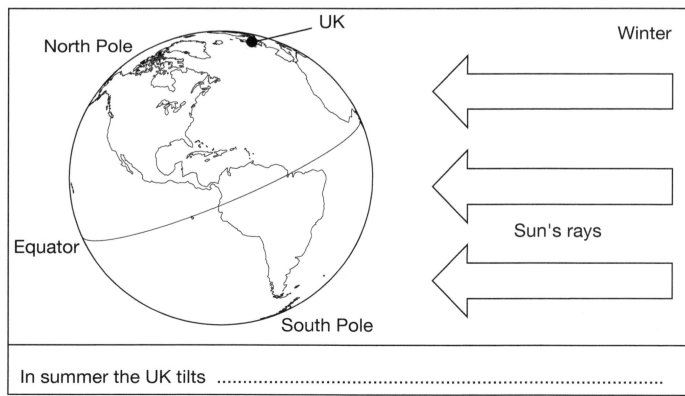

UK

North Pole

Equator

South Pole

Winter

Sun's rays

In summer the UK tilts ....

14 Shelter

1. Colour the house cut-out.

2. Cut along the dotted lines.

3. Glue the model together.

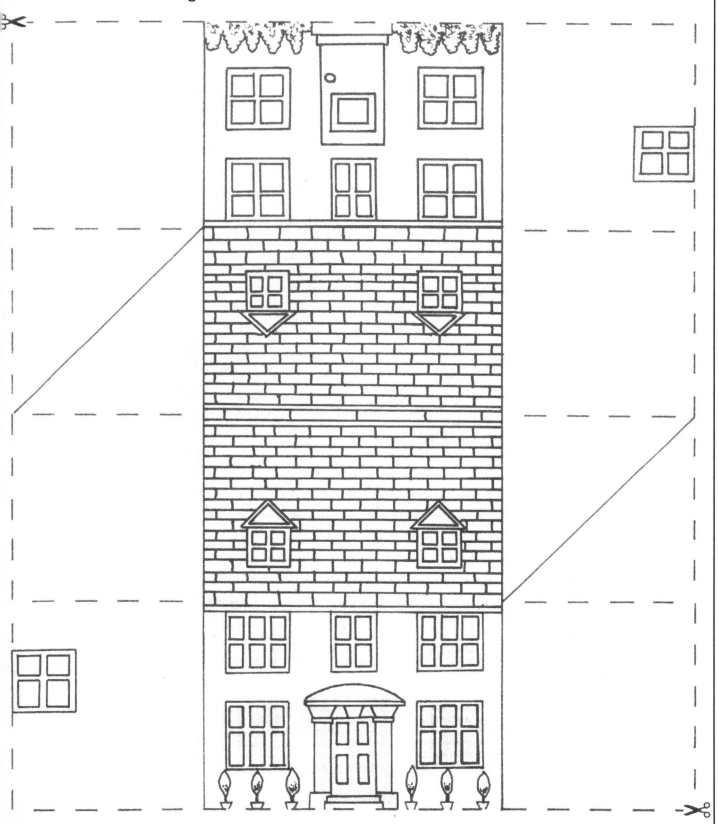

Name ....

1. Colour the pictures.

2. Write the names next to the pictures.

caravan   flats   cottage   stilt-house   terrace   chalet

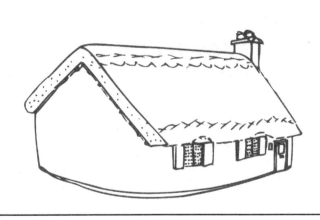

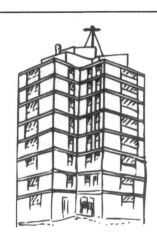

16 Living in a village

Name ....

1. Draw lines from the words to the correct place.

2. Colour the picture.

farm	fields	houses	shop	inn

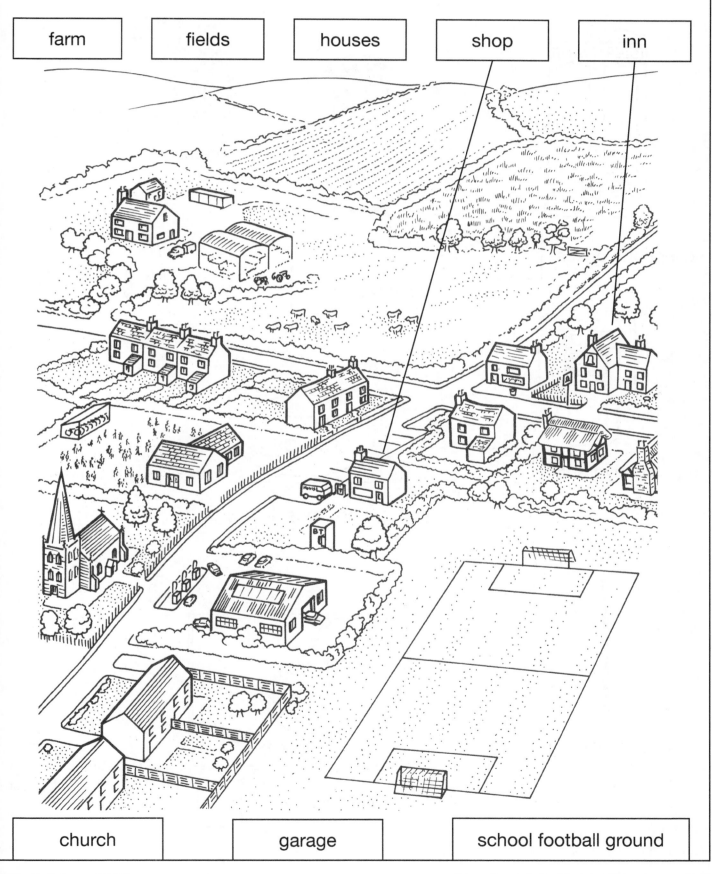

church	garage	school football ground

Name ....

---

1. Go on a local walk. Tick each of these things as you find them.

telephone boxes ☐

post boxes ☐

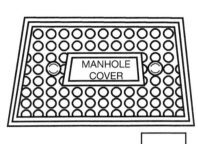

metal covers ☐

drains ☐

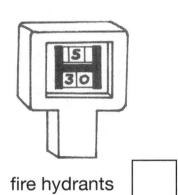

fire hydrants ☐

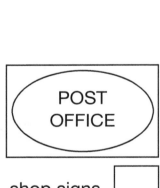

shop signs ☐

overhead wires ☐

advertisements ☐

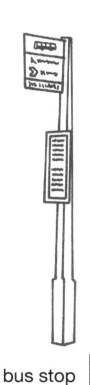

bus stop ☐

Name ....

1. Colour the pictures.

2. Cut round the edge and fold along the dotted line.

3. Glue down the tab to make a street model.

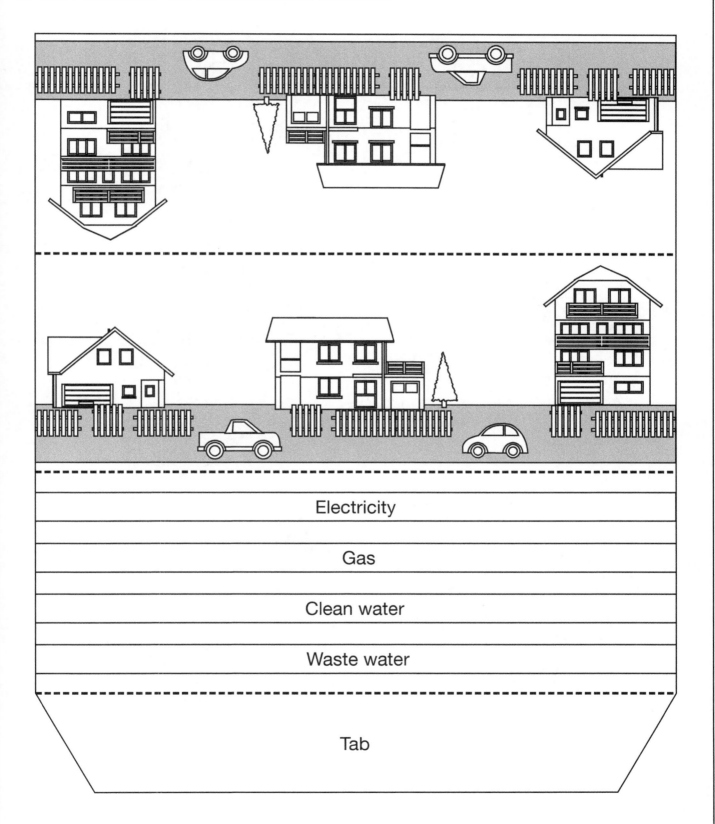

Electricity

Gas

Clean water

Waste water

Tab

Name ....

1. Colour the picture of the hare and tortoise race.

2. How many creatures are watching the race? ....

Name ....

1. Write down the grid square for the castle and the church.

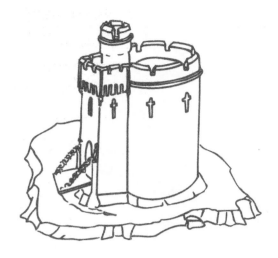

The castle is in

grid square _____

The church is in

grid square _____

2. Make a drawing of one of the things from these grid squares.

Grid square A1	Grid square D2

1. Draw a line from each picture to the right plan.

2. Colour the pictures and plans.

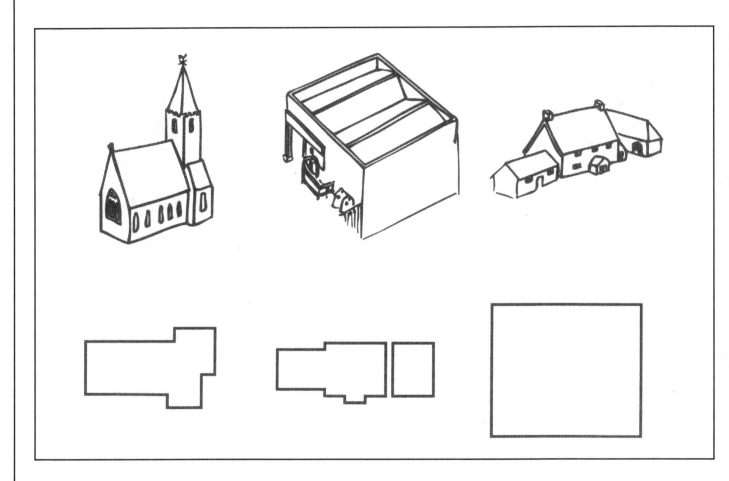

3. Draw a plan of this bungalow.

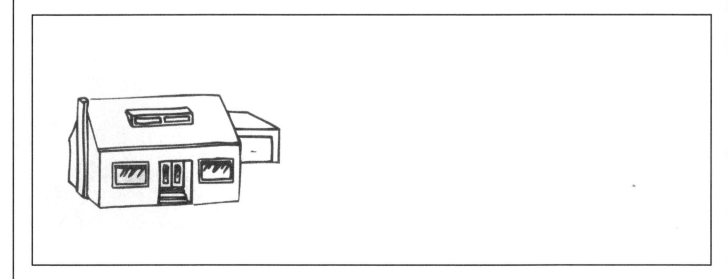

Name ....

1. Make up your own map looking down from above. You could show buildings, roads, rivers, forests. Add other things as you think of them.

	A	B	C	D
5				
4				
3				
2				
1				

Name ....

1. Colour the map using a different colour for each country.

2. Add the name of each country to the map.

3. Colour the flag.

Name ....

1. Colour the UK map.

2. Cut the map into six pieces, muddle them up and put them together.

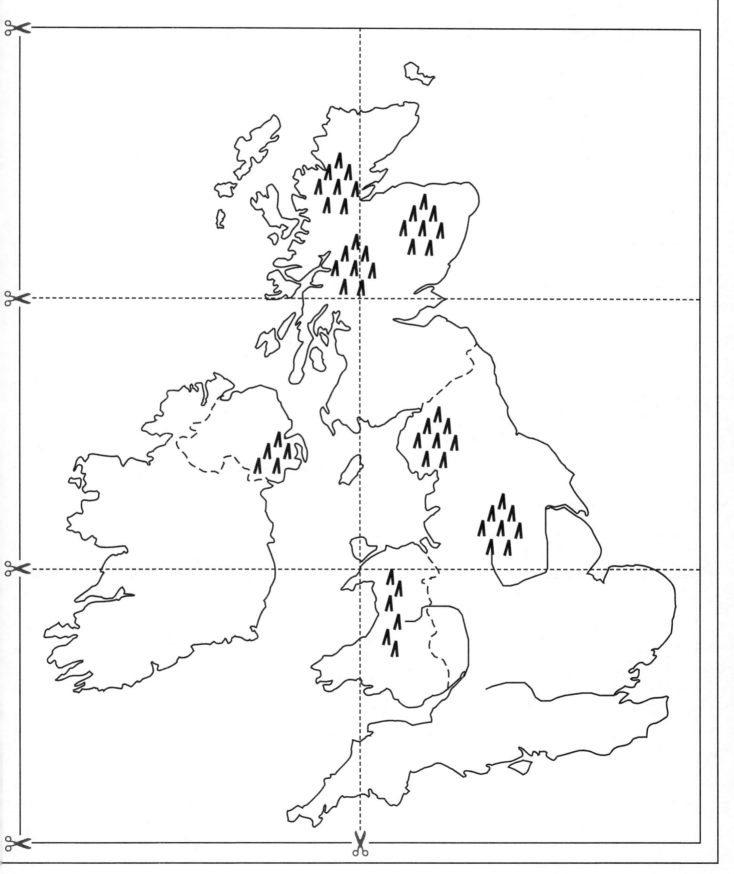

1. Colour the arctic plants and animals.

polar bear	reindeer
walrus	fish
flowers	moss	lichen

Name ....

1. Colour the pictures of the rainforest creatures.

2. Cut them out.

3. Use them on a large rainforest picture of your own.

parrot

butterfly

crocodile

leopard

monkey

turtle

1. Work with other children to make your own drawings for a desert mobile.

1. Join the dots to make the pictures.

2. Name the animals.

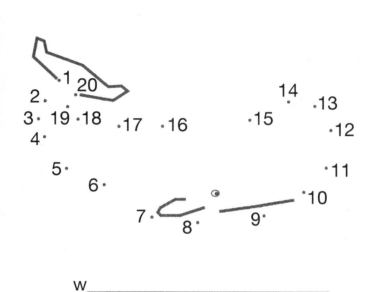

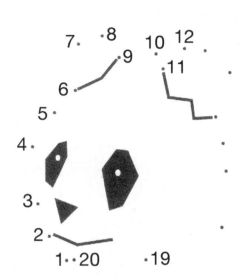

w_____

_____

3. Fit the names of the animals into this crossword.

29 World continents

1. Colour the boxes in the key.

2. Colour the continents using these colours.

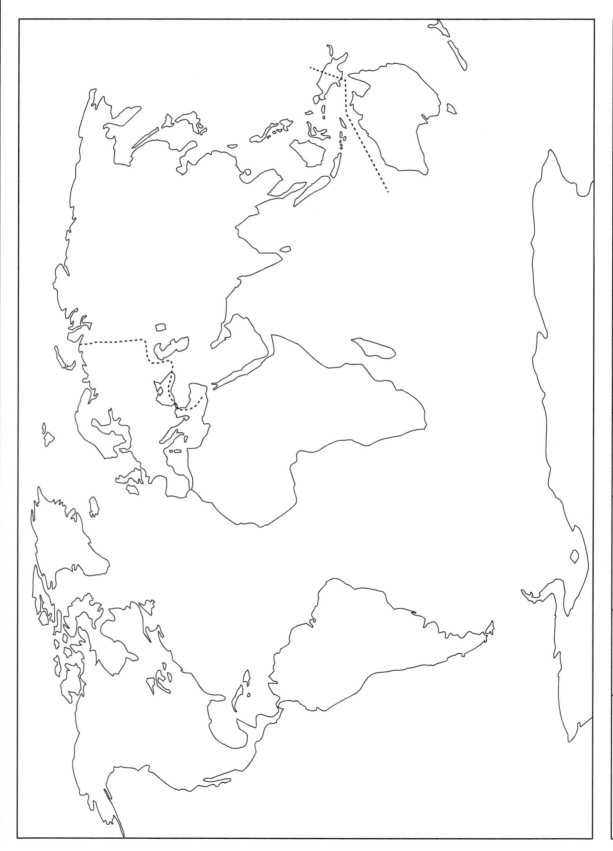

North America	green	Europe	black	Asia	yellow	Antarctica	purple
South America	brown	Africa	red	Oceania	orange		

Name ....

1. Colour the flags and name the countries.

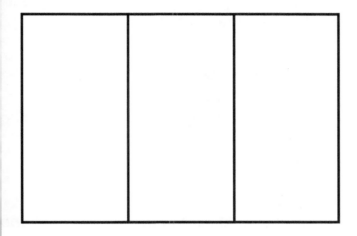

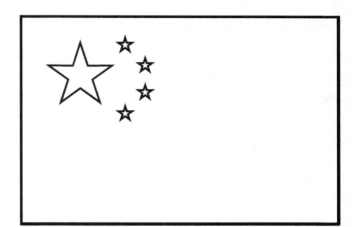

_____

_____

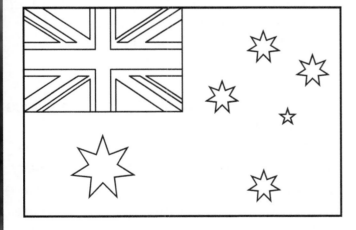

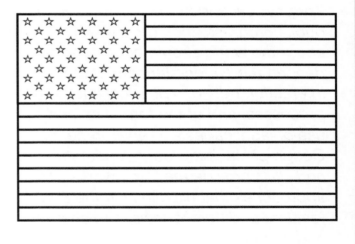

_____

_____

Geography in the English National Curriculum

A new primary geography curriculum was introduced in England in 2014. This new curriculum provides a framework for schools to follow but leaves teachers considerable scope to select and organise the content according to their individual needs. It should also be noted that the curriculum is only intended to occupy a proportion of the school day and that schools are free to devise their own studies in the time that remains.

Purpose of study

The aim of geographical education is clearly articulated in the opening section of the Programme of Study which states:

A high quality geography education should inspire in pupils a curiosity and fascination about the world and its people that will remain with them for the rest of their lives. Teaching should equip pupils with knowledge about diverse places, people, resources and natural and human environments, together with a deep understanding of the Earth's key physical and human processes. As pupils progress, their growing knowledge about the world should help them to deepen their understanding of the interaction between physical and human processes, and of the formation and use of landscapes and environments. Geographical knowledge, understanding and skills provide the frameworks and approaches that explain how the Earth's features at different scales are shaped and interconnected and change over time.

Subject content

The National Curriculum provides the following general guidance for each Key Stage:

Key Stage 1
Pupils should develop knowledge about the world, the United Kingdom and their locality. They should understand basic subject-specific vocabulary relating to human and physical geography and begin to use geographical skills, including first-hand observation, to enhance their locational awareness.

Key Stage 2
Pupils should extend their knowledge and understanding beyond the local area to include the United Kingdom and Europe, North and South America. This will include the location and characteristics of a range of the world's most significant human and physical features. They should develop their use of geographical knowledge, understanding and skills to enhance their locational and place knowledge.

Teachers who are familiar with the previous version of the curriculum will note the increasing emphasis on factual and place knowledge. For example, there is a greater focus on learning about the UK and Europe. Map reading and communication skills are also highlighted. On the other hand, there are no specific references to the developing world and sustainability is not mentioned directly. However, there is an expectation that schools will work from the Programmes of Study to develop a broad and balanced curriculum which meets the needs of learners in their locality. This provides schools with scope to enrich the curriculum and rectify any omissions which they may perceive.

Key Stage 1 Programme of study

The elements specified in the Key Stage 1 programme of study are listed below. The summary provided here should read alongside the statements about the wider aims of the curriculum. There is no suggestion that pupils or teachers should work to individual statements.

Key Stage 1 Geography National Curriculum
Develop knowledge about the world
Develop knowledge about the UK
Develop knowledge about their locality
Locational knowledge
Name and locate the seven continents
Name and locate the five oceans
Name and locate the four countries of the UK
Name and locate the capital cities of the four UK countries
Name and locate the seas surrounding the UK
Place knowledge
Physical and human geography of a small area of the UK
Physical and human geography of a small area of a contrasting non-European country
Human and physical geography
Identify seasonal weather patterns in the UK
Identify daily weather patterns in the UK
Identify location of hot areas of the world
Identify location of cold areas of the world
Identify the Equator and North and South Poles
Use basic vocabulary to refer to physical features
Use basic vocabulary to refer to human features
Geographical skills and fieldwork
Use world maps, atlases and globes
Use simple compass directions
Use directional and locational language
Identify features and routes on a map
Use aerial photos and plan perspectives
Devise a simple map
Use and construct basic symbols in a key
Use simple fieldwork and observational skills in their school, its grounds and surroundings

WORLD MAP

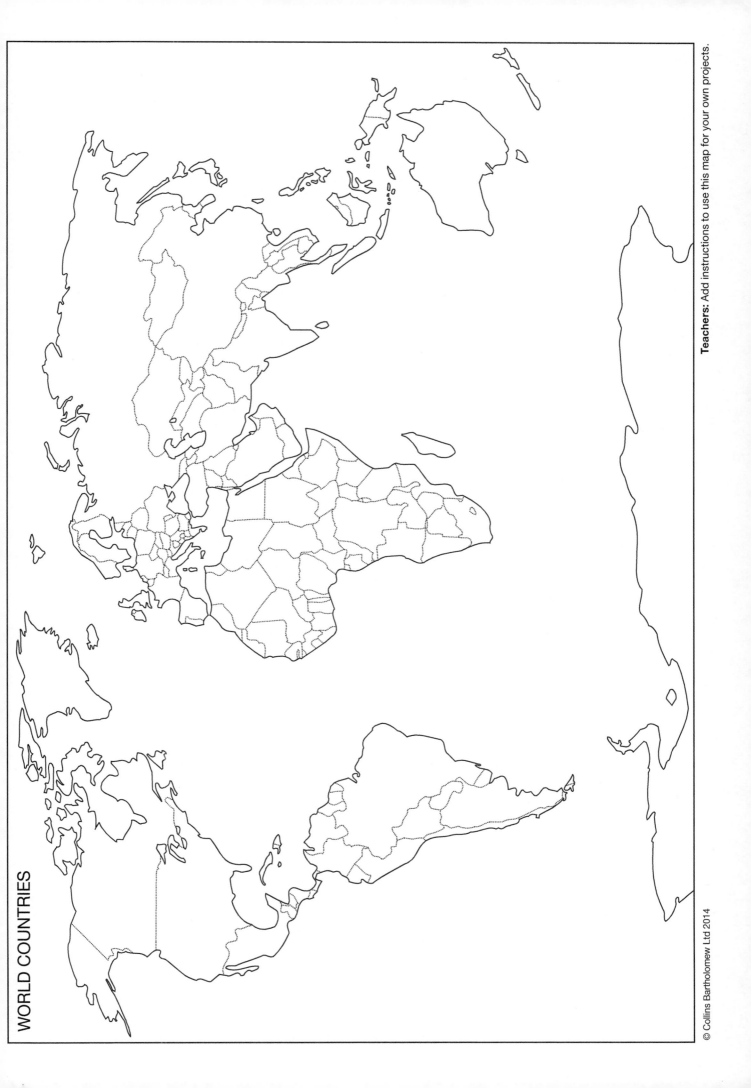

WORLD COUNTRIES

Teachers: Add instructions to use this map for your own projects.

Published by Collins
An imprint of HarperCollins Publishers
Westerhill Road
Bishopbriggs
Glasgow G64 2QT

www.harpercollins.co.uk

HarperCollins*Publishers*
1st Floor, Watermarque Building, Ringsend Road
Dublin 4, Ireland

First edition 2014

A catalogue record for this book is available from the British Library.

ISBN 978-0-00-756363-0

20 19 18 17 16 15

Printed and Bound in the UK using 100% Renewable Electricity at CPI Group (UK) Ltd

Most of the mapping in this publication is generated from Collins Bartholomew digital databases. Collins
Bartholomew, the UK's leading independent geographical information supplier, can provide a digital,
custom, and premium mapping service to a variety of markets.
For further information: Tel: +44 (0)208 307 4515
e-mail: collinsbartholomew@harpercollins.co.uk

Visit our websites at:
www.collins.co.uk
www.collinsbartholomew.com

Acknowledgements

Cover designs Steve Evans illustration and design

Photo credits:

All images from www.shutterstock.com